midnight writers

First Published in India in 2020

Inkfeathers Publishing

New Delhi 110095

Copyright © Inkfeathers Publishing, 2020

Cover Design © 2020 Inkfeathers Publishing

Cover Image by © Cliford Mervil from Pexels

www.inkfeathers.com

midnight writers

a collection of the finest poetry

Edited & Compiled by

Muskan Srivastava

Inkfeathers Publishing

Co-Authored By

Rashi Agarwal ~ Dr. Apteena Johnson Kakkadu ~
Fiza Meghrajiya ~ Sushma Chaudhary ~ Anushka Shah ~
Arshveen Behr ~ Manoj Vaz ~ Tanvi Kulkarni ~ Sehaf Haq ~
Saniya Rumaiza ~ Jagruthi Kommuri ~ Padmini Peteri ~
Madhurya Kommuri ~ Joe King ~ Prakriti Batra ~ Mrinalini
Singh ~ Shrishail Bhurke ~ Keshav Dev Tiwari ~ Pranshi Singal
~ Laiba Sohail ~ John McCafferty ~ Utkarsh Pandey ~ Priya
Kulkarni ~ Deeksha Raina ~ Purva Mestry Ingale ~ Ethan
Chinnery ~ Kristina Kerber ~ Alexandra Michelle ~ Kunika
Rawlani ~ Chris Scully ~ Nandana Nataraj ~ Ruchika Sharma ~
Vaishnavi Singh ~ C.L. Williams ~ Manaswi Patil ~ Snehal
Agarwal

CONTENTS

ABOUT THE EDITOR

Muskan Srivastava

Born in the laps of Uttar Pradesh, Muskan Srivastava is a 20- year-old currently pursuing her graduation in Computer Science. Defining her as an introvert might be a swanky affair but none can pull her out from the fantasies and whims of the little world she has created around herself.

Little did she know there was a writer hiding inside her when one day, three years back, she took her pen and wrote a poem for her mother. The beauty of words descended upon her so easily that, with her new discovery, she hardly ever stopped scribbling away.

The world is not black and white and she doesn't see a reason why her fictional worlds must be written as such, so she writes on a range of genres including poetry, mystery, etc. Be what it may be, she puts her soul in whatever she does and doesn't let anyone and anything come in her way of success. She believes that writing is an exploration - you start from nothing and learn as you go along. Apart from writing, Muskan loses herself gaily in dancing and actively takes part in social works in an attempt to spread love. Rather than pretending to be perfect, she puts her heart in whatever she does to be flawless.

EDITOR'S NOTE

The book 'Midnight Writers' is not just a book, it's my dream - a dream that helped me achieve greater heights in the field of writing, helped me peek into the rare perspectives of people and groove their words in the most interesting way.

The experience that compiling this book gave me is amazing beyond words with each step of the production process creating a flutter of memories and excitement for the impending success.

In about 81 poems ranging in their theme, subject, style and characters, our most talented writers offer an unforgettable tapestry of love: vibrant, messy, enigmatic, and enduring.

When I first went through the submissions, I was fascinated by how the writers were viscerally unafraid to be naked on the page, their emotions laying bare without embellishment or embarrassment. They had shown me the power to be vulnerable and would have the same effect on any reader that picks the book.

Love, emotions, dreams, passion, feelings, and beauty can be depicted from the piece of art here. The anthology can be said to be to of a somewhat romantic endeavour: born of youthful idealism, built by the hard work of many people, and kept alive by passion — for the written word, for an honest poem well told, for fragile humanity in all its guises.

Being a voracious reader, the field of poetry has given me so much and Midnight Writers is just a small contribution, a token of love from my side to the field of writing and poetry.

Again, thank you to all who made this publication possible. I simply couldn't have done it without you. Happy reading!

midnight writers

a collection of the finest poetry

The New Beginning

by Rashi Aggarwal

Today, I turned a new leaf,

The fire burning in my soul is finally extinguished.

It did leave burns, it did leave marks.

The damage caused is irreversible, but this doesn't

mean it can't be repaired.

Once upon a time, I was a strong girl,

Hurricane, flood, nothing could knock me down.

But, all of a sudden I found myself surrounded by dark clouds,

The dark clouds of melancholia.

I was lost, fighting each second, to find my way out.

It seemed like all my efforts went in vain.

It felt as if I was thrown into the sea, not knowing how to swim.

I felt suffocated.

There was an avalanche of panic,

And no one was there to save me.

I was alone, all to myself.

No one could save me but I, me and myself.

I pulled myself together and escaped from the cage of utmost

dismay.

I experienced depression, insomnia, loneliness and

self-hatred.

But it failed to break me apart

because today, I turned a new leaf.

Folks of Love

by Dr. Apteena Johnson Kakkadu

"Love"

What a pretty weapon,

it kills,

it cuts,

right through the hearts,

it's painful.

But we never stop loving!

Perhaps,

we'll never know,

that we are dying,

until one day,

when we feel numb and freeze,

both flesh and heart.

Memories often enliven the process,

agonizing and

fiercing the pain,

shades of your face will be flashing,

reminiscing the past,

making me realize,

that I haven't moved on,

still, I'm here,

where you left me with grief and flowers...

Sunset and Moonrise

by Fiza Meghrajiya

As the sun sets and the

beautiful colours explodes

all over the sky,

my pain fades away

just like the colours

while watching it.

As the moon rises

in the darkest night,

my secret talks with

my moon starts too.

It helps me to get

out of my darkest times.

Sunset and moon rise

are truly my happy

places whenever I'm

having my rough days.

The beauty of sunset

never lies and

my secret keeper moon

never betrays.

Millions of places

to travel in world,

But all I'm craving for

is sunset and moon rise.

Glancing Through the Window

by Sushma Chaudhary

She always used to glance through the window

just to see him out,

making many excuses,

she runs throughout the house.

She sits with her favourite novel,

dreaming about the characters as 'we'

but looking at him she gets lost,

just as the pearl in the sea.

Stars

by Anushka Shah

I do believe in your galaxy,

The stars in your Milky Way,

How will they appear in your sky?

Don't forget that I found you anyways,

At the end of my despair.

You're the last reason,

For me who was standing at the edge of the cliff, to live.

The Sky is Pink

by Arshveen Behr

You snuck out,

At the falling of the day,

To meet him,

Under the sky so grey,

You stood there,

In the middle of the ground,

With your hair blowing,

By the wind around,

You kept gazing,

In his eyes so deep,

And let your soul talk,

About the things you couldn't speak,

He held your hand,

You felt your ear blush,

And pulled you closer,

And said with a hush,

Meet me again,

Again somewhere,

Out in the lands,

Where the love we share,

You'll know when it's time,

You'll know what to think.

Meet me again,

When, the sky is pink.

The Stranger

by Manoj Vaz

An unknown land bare and rundown,
And I met a stranger there.
Faces all around, known unknown,
And I met my stranger there.

A crowd I missed to walk alone,
in the dark near the lake somewhere.
No fear, no thoughts, no sins to atone,
And I was with my stranger there.

Laughter, tears, tears of laughter,
While, ego played the game of vain.
A smile, a nod, a wink, a gesture,
And there I met my stranger again.

The strange softly became familiar,
The long drives, the never-ending walks.
He held his dark hand on mine so fair,
The warm hugs, the heart-to-heart talks.

The moment still, the stars bright,

A bright light shone; I closed my eyes.

My stranger disappeared into my night,

I cried, I begged for tender mercies.

A strange dream that make tears recur,

A strange wish for longing love remain.

A strange urge to kiss him forever,

Knowing I will never see my stranger again.

Blur of Motion

by Tanvi Kulkarni

<hr>

When the blur of motion will cease,

only the graveyard of suppressed emotion,

will be left to appease.

At whom will you so hatefully scorn,

when you realize all are forlorn?

Shadows will henceforth exist,

where, drizzled joy's heavenly mist.

Existence will be as empty as a dirge,

with no soul left to purge.

Of its sins,

All that's left will be pins.

Pins of forgotten "what if's",

so foolishly trying to scour clean,

All the past tiff's,

Trying to regain the fractured "has been"

Fractured pieces of the invincible mind,

Fallen from its Herculean might,

some left behind,

in uncertainty's darkest night.

The Walk

by Rashi Aggarwal

I still remember the walk I took,

After school, towards the forest.

The magnificent beauty in every nook,

Mesmerized me like a song to a chorist.

The trees, the grass, and the flowers

were looking so beautiful.

Seemed like blissful showers,

under which hours could be delightful.

Tantalizing spell of bountiful nature,

I got disturbed by the ring of my duties,

Telling me to watch my time and be mature,

Confronted by real-life cruelties.

At that point, the bitter dogma was realized,

Life is a race and many are to be beaten.

There is no time for things to be relished,

Save yourselves from being eaten.

Dusk to Dawn

by Priya Kulkarni

Playing with her tresses,

the sheet and its ceases.

Their story begins,

and ends with nothing.

He traps her in his arms,

where she's locked until dawn.

Their love for each other,

goes on until dusk & dawn....

Why I Love Sunsets

by Sehaf Haq

The evening has fallen as is its routine,
a beautiful scene unfolds, the sky a screen.

From my perch on the sands of the beach,
I watch as the sun turns into a blend of coral and peach.

Its colours slowly seep out and around it like dye,
and then there are pink, purple and red waves in the sky.

The waves envelope the clouds in a sweet caress,
that look like cotton candy, and nothing less.

As the sun disappears, the screen turns inky blue,
with all their beauty, the stars come through.

The darkness that spreads reminds me,
of the darkness that resides within me.

I remember how it grew and thickened,

filled with dead silence for those who listened.

But it never came with a setting sun,

nor was there hope of a rising one.

To escape this darkness with no beginning, nor an end,

I sit by the beach everyday, to watch another of its kind.

Twilight Love

by Saniya Rumaiza

In the growing hour of the ticking clock,

I reminisced about our late-night walk.

Bruised and dusted I came along,

to sing to your glory, our cradled love's song.

The shadowy moon;

your smile as a boon;

the swaying trees;

the refreshing breeze;

the footsteps underneath which everything bloomed;

twilight sky and the midnight gloom.

Centuries ago, sang the stars,

the story of our love on my behalf.

Misinterpretation of the lust in our eyes,

ignorance of the buts', how's and why's.

We became the gem of the talking bunch,

detecting our boundaries was their wildest hunch.

The stars sang, the fish swam by,

and in the awakening of our love,

I somehow felt alive.

First Rain

by Jagruthi Kommuri

She is like the first droplets of rain,

Soothing away the heaviness of the pain;

(Pure as a little baby's smile, yet insane)

She is the sound of the drizzle after a long sunny season,

Gives a hope that every yearning has a reason;

She is like the cool breeze after a mist,

A sense of happiness but with a twist;

She is the smell of mud after the first rain fell,

Couldn't deny but accept being under her spell.

From Time to Time

by Padmini Peteri

From time to time,

Do you think about me?

Do you miss me?

Do you dream about me?

I dream about you every other day,

I dream about,

the beautiful gaze you own.

I dream about,

your fingers running through my hair.

I dream about the scent you leave on the sheets,

I dream about the conversations we had,

I dream about

all the dreams we dreamt,

the promises you broke,

the scars you gave,

and all the pain I suffer,

I dreamt about

our love blooming like a flower,

but in reality it withered like a flower!

The Waves and I

by Sehaf Haq

The waves and I,

we sing the same song,

we lament separation from the shore,

from stability, from moments of rest,

we thrash in terror of the horrors,

that lie deep within our bellies,

but mostly we just run, and run,

for if we stayed too still,

the dirt of our and others' sins would rise

and make itself known to the world,

the lives we harbour in our bosoms,

will cease to exist,

so we ignore our exhaustion,

and continue to dance to the moon.

What is Love?

by Madhurya Kommuri

It is as simple as my heart when it found you,

as complicated as my mind when it thinks of losing you.

Love is when my heart skipped a beat,

when I saw you for the first time,

It's when I fell for you deeper walking by your side.

It's when people say "Have you lost your mind?" when they see me

daydreaming about you.

It's when I found my true courageous self, fighting for you.

Love is when your look took my breath away.

It's when your touch breathe

life into my broken pieces.

It's a mystery as deep as your eyes,

it's the answer I found in your smile.

Love is when my quest ended when you held my hand,

and my pursuit to hold it forever began.

Confused Soul

by Jagruthi Kommuri

When we are kids we want to grow fast,

When we are young we wish if we could last,

And in old age we sit and regret our past;

When we are single we wait to mingle,

When we are in love we wish be to single;

We don't know why our hearts flutter and tingle;

When we have nothing we wish we had something,

When we have something we wish we had everything,

But someday we'll know everything is nothing;

We wish we had chance to choose,

Sometimes we gain nothing but lose,

Yet this restless soul is left confused.

The Burden of Love

by Joe King

I think about you for hours a day,

A day in the life of an I.N.F.J

I'm in my own way, and I'm blocking my view.

As thoughts blind my eyes when I'm thinking of you,

And without even knowing, you've conquered my mind.

My head is now spinning, and my eyes have gone blind,

And when you say "Hey", my spirits have risen,

But when you're away, my heart's stuck in prison.

My mind is erratic, and it's hard to express,

Some days I'm ecstatic, and on others depressed.

My heart is a slave, and it feels underpowered,

It wants to be saved, but runs like a coward.

Those three little words could just change my life,

They could bring me a soulmate, and even a wife.

But I don't play this game, as I've already lost,

As my heart tells my brain, "Anxiety's the boss."

My Kind of Love

by Prakriti Batra

Wasn't it love that made me stare?

Wasn't it care that made me stay?

It's like the way things have been,

that makes me crave the heart break to feel the love again.

I was making him happy effortlessly,

Then I had to make efforts.

It was hard at first,

The dark clouds wouldn't go away.

I kept chasing the rainbow,

But it seems all I needed was the rain.

We are just people,

With big hearts and fewer words.

Grooming ourselves to be in a better state,

All we wouldn't be is the same kind of love.

Bits of Love

by Mrinalini Singh

They were like a rosy couple,

But nobody saw the thorns they had hidden,

Beneath their petals of love,

They were like the sun so bright together,

But none felt the heat between them,

They were like the moon shining,

But only if people you knew they shined,

to keep the darkness away,

Love is great and there is no doubt about it,

It requires passion, strength and sacrifice,

which they did to keep their love alive,

even after their death,

Today it lives in the hearts of those who witnessed it.

Life Goes On

by Jagruthi Kommuri

This moment, it soon becomes a memory,

Recapture happy times before you understand life is temporary;

A friend someday might become a stranger,

Don't let love end because of a minute's anger;

Your grief will one day be healed,

Your lie, it definitely gets revealed;

People like seasons may change,

Be yourself, let world assume you're strange;

Present will become future's history,

Life even till the last breath is a mystery;

Today will become tomorrow's yesterday,

Learn to Live, Love and Laugh anyway.

Love Has No Assurance

by Mrinalini Singh

The fear of losing someone

so close was the same

as of a kid sleeping without a mother,

Being with him was a risk like.

an adventure without precautions,

there was no assurance of.

What was going to happen next?

Do Not Expect

by Jagruthi Kommuri

If you care, and they don't, be kind,

Do not expect from an empty cup being blind;

If you miss, and they don't, find ways your love can still be expressed,

Do not expect the world to be loyal, it is already enough depressed;

If you forgive, and they don't forget, forgive even more,

Do not expect they will change, it's the game of ego just ignore;

If you love, and they don't, do not love less,

Love is not a give and take business.

Never presume this universe works as you expected,

Remember life is all about living the unexpected.

The Eyes Say it All

by Shrishail Bhurke

A look into those eyes,

And I drown deep into them,

Things silent whispers couldn't reveal,

And the eyes say it all....

Those eyes devoid of sleep,

Keeping you awake in the nights so deep,

Though you try hiding your every emotion,

The eyes say it all....

Just a glance at those droopy eyes,

And all the memories prevail,

Silence fell in every corner,

Yet, the eyes say it all....

Your gleaming eyes, the stars mimic and dazzle,

How could I ever let them dull?

Your lips are quiet but,

The eyes say it all...

I'd Loved You Enough to Let You Go

by Keshav Dev Tiwari

You are my deepest desire,

because darling you and only you

suits my attire...

I remember, the day we met,

I was crazy,

Our eyes were drowning in one another,

and you were looking dazzling...

That's your shoulder where I want to lay down,

when you are the queen and I want to wear the crown...

The moments that we made, shared and cherished signifies our eternal love and

care...

The intimacy that grew between us,

I want to keep that alive

so that one fine day, down on my knee...

Asking you for the best part,

"Let's turn us into we so that no-one can put us apart...."

But I know, these are just dreams which

will just leave one day

in my voice as screams...

I'll be living my life alone,

I'll not be holding your hand

but my love that's not the end...

I'll always water, the tree of our love,

It will always shine with your natural charm.

But let me tell you something darling,

I'd loved you enough,

to let you go.....

Letting You Go

by Pranshi Singal

Lovesick by your intriguing eyes,

that took me to a place where heaven lies,

those barriers between us built by fate,

is tearing my heart.

Like its best trait,

I wanna spread my wings to soar high,

Let go of everything without any sigh,

the way I became yours parted me from myself.

The intensity of this love,

became limitless...

But now, as you left leaving me all alone,

only as a memory,

left for me to cherish,

but perished me,

it pulls me apart,

it breaks my heart,

but I can still love you,

and let you go.

Unrequited Love

by Laiba Sohail

As he looks at me,

and watches me stutter,

He encourages me to say it all;

Say it with clarity and finality,

But I can't,

Because I don't want him to hear those words,

I want someone else to be all ears for.

Divorce

by Laiba Sohail

She watched her house burnt down,
She didn't know what to do.
She watched the flowers turn black;
Once, a deep shade of blue.
She watched and watched but didn't cry,
As, the fire wasn't new.
That was something insidious;
Burnt her all through...
Made her question what she knew.

When the Sky Cried with Me

by Sehaf Haq

‿‿‿‿‿‿‿‿‿‿‿‿‿‿‿‿‿‿‿‿‿‿‿‿‿‿‿‿‿‿‿‿‿‿‿‿‿

My heart is like the dark sky before the rain,

laden with clouds that are brimming with your memories,

and when they burst, they soak me in pain.

My heartbeats sound like the stormy downpour,

thundering against my rib cage,

for they are still in sync with the song of your soul.

My soul has fallen into an abyss as dark as the sky,

it quivers, not in cold but in nostalgia,

all it can recall from the past is your goodbye.

Today the sky cried with me, after a summer of forever,

digging up memories a billion years old,

it was a beautiful affair, when our tears fell together.

But today's rainfall was the means of a fresh start,

for when we stopped crying, there was a rainbow

not just in the sky, but also in my heart.

Limbo

by John McCafferty

Stuck in a moment,

temporarily on hold,

How long to forgo alone?

Searching in haste through space,

though the globe still spins,

our world has slowed.

No hairline cracks but open gaps,

in broken moulds.

A collective directive,

or tall order from top to bottom,

Who sets the tone?

With answers unknown,

Not the forgotten.

So my friend,

educate yourself and

be bold as you bend,

To the weight of the world.

We are All Sailors

by Utkarsh Pandey

Handful life, emotions raging.

Set of experiences, calibrating.

At the moment here and now.

But also, dreaming and longing.

You feel it's always less.

Creating preferences over, alignments.

Time slips more each day, confinements.

You deliberate to the visions.

People dawdle, frivolously.

You shatter hindrances, vigorously.

As the distance covered will matter.

A great life lived within, will scatter,

Peace, happiness and love.

Love won't Last

by Priya Kulkarni

You tie it down,

It goes where

it is free to roam around.

Love is loyal,

Don't dare to doubt it,

Freedom keeps a healthy space,

Between you & me.

Distance always closes,

Which is there between us,

We do not tie down,

And then call it our own.

You

by Jagruthi Kommuri

I search for you in every person I meet,

Isn't it funny how one person can make you feel complete?

You were the distance I wouldn't mind to walk,

My journey with you will forever be special to talk;

Each new day you seem to be a new story,

I would like to read and unveil the glory;

You are somewhere miles away yet very near,

Why is love so strange to express and hence I fear;

You might think you are just like any other person one can find,

I want you to know that you are one in a million kind;

Words could limit in describing what you mean to me,

But I hope someday you will definitely see.

Hope

by Jagruthi Kommuri

Hope... because it keeps us going,

Hope... because it helps us growing.

It doesn't make things easy,

But it sure does make you believe the impossible,

And you know what, hope will one day make things possible;

It will test your faith at times,

But it is what that brings us together,

Hope gives us courage to help each other;

It will one day challenge love,

At times when you are drowning in doubt,

And you'll know hope is what made you try it out;

It may seem like everyone is changing,

And everything around you is falling apart,

Then hope is the only thing that aids in surviving till last;

Hope... because it makes life worth living.

Hope... because it helps us keep trying.

Broken Bands

by Deeksha Raina

The first time we met,

The air carried an aura of awkwardness,

Didn't linger much, we didn't,

Crossed paths only to say goodbye.

Fate tossed a coin instead,

We were supposed to be friends, it said,

That day we struck a deal, you and me,

Cautiously stepped into the fleet of ships,

Naming it with our synced dreams,

The slanting fonts, our mirrored idiosyncrasies.

We fought our battles together,

Our thoughts were the propeller,

Sailing through the storm we endured,

I was at the helm, you were my captain.

The thunderous clouds parted ways,

To welcome a pirate on our deck,

The blackness of his patch

Directed the course of our ship,

Drowning in testing waters,

In a cacophony of lies and shame.

The hull lay broken,

The emotions now snapped,

That one time we met,

I could almost taste the salts,

Didn't linger much, we didn't,

Crossed paths only to say goodbye.

Someday

by Purva Mestry Ingale

It's late, very late.

But, is it?

I know it may be a misunderstanding or just miscommunication.

Or is it?

Life is short and there are boundaries.

But weren't they always there?

Does your entrance in my life change anything?

Does it bring me the freedom I crave?

Does it take away the loneliness I face?

I am happy, but not complete.

I hope I get the freedom I crave.

I hope I live my life my way some day!

Our Goodbyes

by Ethan Chinnery

Dust hangs in the air,

As if for a moment you came back here.

The dust dances as I reach out for your hand,

Alas! You aren't here anymore...

You were just an apparition of sunlit dust,

A ghost of memories,

Haunting me with moments,

Those cherished.

Those regrettable words,

Our moments,

How I miss our clumsy cooking,

Those quiet movie nights,

The times we played like the children we once where,

Looking around our house,

Not a house but a home,

A place built on our time together...

I regretfully realise now I must bid you farewell,

Tears flow down my cheek,

As I pack our things in ragged boxes,

Every object becoming a road to see you again,

A road which I'll never be able to travel and be with you again...

As I turn over your photo in my hand, I realise now, all I am left with is

memories of us...

Without Me

by Priya Kulkarni

I heard my heart scream in protest,

Against the break which it felt

I tried to not feel the pain,

I tried taking the pain away,

But it was determined to stay,

Refusing to budge or sway,

Watching you walk away

Seeing my life walking away.

I tried taking the pain away,

Without you in my Life

I knew that I would never be the same again.

The Joys you gave also refused to stay,

Walking behind you instead,

I tried taking the pain away.

Let me hug one last time,

Give you all that I had called mine.

Hoping that it maybe all I can give,

Happiness it is nothing else at all,

This is the last gift of remembrance from my side,

Wishing you nothing but happiness…

In the life you would live.

Without me…

Adoration

by Kristina Kerber

The sun caresses my cheeks

While the wind gently kisses my forehead,

I remember the island as we go by,

But all I can feel is your ardent ocean

Delicately dancing within my tranquil chest.

There's no sky or sea or soil,

Just your adoring arms

Warily wrapped around my weightless waist

Like a fire shielding me from the ashes,

Completely engulfing me in your flames,

Burning away the darkness of my mind,

Cleansing me of myself

Until I'm pure again.

And all this worry and fear trapped inside me

Comes crashing down with the waves

Until all that I am

Is sunlight and wind

In your arms...

Courage

by Deeksha Raina

They ask you, why writing

And you just shudder,

Shudder at their question

Or your answer?

It's times like this,

When you are sitting in the quiet

And yet the voices echo within

The brain, quiet a complicated organ

Yes, you blame it on the cerebral

You chastise it for keeping still,

when it should have been kicking in,

It's like, that drug affects

when you least expect it to,

Yes it's the brain at fault, your brain.

Or maybe, you just don't have it,

Maybe, you lack the very fibre in your bone.

Or wait!

What if it's the voice!?

You know you're speaking these words,

These very words that you dare to write

Yet your tongue seems,

To recoil in the larynx when needed

And so you sit mum, head down,

And the voices you hear are not your own.

Maybe, you just don't have it,

Just maybe, you lack the very fibre in your bone.

Quietly you stand,

as decisions are taken on your behalf

Your eyes, they scream

The words just ready to burst,

Anytime now,

bubbling in the buds of your tongue,

Finally, you hear the words,

you hear what you want to say

Or do you?

Blinking your eyes, you drown your screams

into the unspeakable pool of your silenced voice

Maybe, you just don't have it.

When he tiptoed towards you,

your thoughts – they ran wild

he touched you

and you engulfed your denial in the dark

You didn't want to ruin his place,

and you even forgave.

When you were kissed, by another man

You didn't close your eyes,

Yet your lips, they remain sealed

You believed what he wanted you to,

Were you raped, or was it virgin luck

You aren't sure and so you think,

You didn't want to be proven wrong

and so you move on.

Or maybe, you just don't have it.

You even tried to escape,

you read about the many ways,

Yet you shun this weakness,

as you tell yourself,

And so you thought it best to quit

Quit from quitting, or so you think

Or maybe, you just don't have it.

And so you write,

Because you find yourself,

exploding, on the edge

And yet if someone asks,

You'll continue to shudder

Or worse,

for you have,

already prepared an answer

Rephrased it, over and again

To every question,

you will have the perfect answer,

Fitting in into the slabs of society.

Or maybe, you just lack the very fibre in your bone.

Love Affair

by Alexandra Michelle

everything intensifies during

a full moon. your edge creeps

up slowly on the awaiting shore.

steady build up as you fill her

with your depths. rhythmically,

you ebb and flow as you explore.

wave after wave crash upon her,

until she reaches high tide. she is

submerged but always wants more.

foaming, you recede into yourself.

glowing in moonlight, she awaits the

next tide as you swell for an encore.

love affair between the ocean and shore.

Revelation

by Laiba Sohail

The time when the sun is about to set,

And the darkness is about to rise,

The silence that seems to fall,

Makes me wonder,

If, this is the time...

When nature tries to whisper her secrets,

That we fail to hear.

One Day I Will Hold You

by Joe King

When, your heart is feeling down,

And there's no one else around.

My words will wrap around you,

Then you feel my love surround you.

If your heart is feeling empty,

I shall fill it up aplenty,

I shall do this all with words.

Till your heart no longer hurts,

And if you're feeling worthless

I will send you many verses,

With words that say, "You're Special"

Then you see your full potential,

So don't forget this poem,

As my heart for you is glowing,

And one day I WILL hold you…

So remember what I've told you…

Yours Forever… Joe

Divine Sign

by Jagruthi Kommuri

I look at the moon, it reminds me of your serene face,

Just as it lights up the night, you ignite my darkest space;

I look at the stars, they remind me of your sparkling eyes,

Just as they twinkle and befriend the lonely sky, you help me illuminate and

empathize;

I look at the sun, it reminds me of your angelic smile,

Just as it warms a winter morning, you make life's adventures worthwhile;

I look at the flying birds, they remind me of your wavy hair,

Just as they flutter by and bring joy, when you are around, love is in the air

I look at the roaring ocean, it reminds me of your melodious voice,

Just as it gives solace to the soul, you have become my hearts rejoice;

I look at this vast universe, every detail of God's marvellous design,

While everything reminds me of you, every little thing about you reminds me of

God, because I believe you are his Divine Sign.

Mirror and Me

by Kunika Rawlani

Mirror mirror on the wall,

Do you also think I look too small?

Mirror mirror on the wall,

What do you think I am, overall?

Mirror mirror on the wall,

Do you think,

What I am right now is right at all?

Mirror mirror on the wall,

Do I think too small?

Mirror on the wall,

Speaks,

Dear girl,

No I don't think you are too small,

Because size of heart is all.

I think you are great overall.

If it feels right,

Then it is my dear.

No dear, you don't think too small,

You wander with your thoughts,

That's why you are asking these doubts.

Hourglass

by Nandana Nataraj

I watch the fine sand grains trickling through those curves.

An undying beauty–she stood over the wooden, worn out table.

Gazing through the antique hourglass epitomizing time,

a random question shot through my mind.

Are my days dropping down, just like the sand oozing down?

Slowly did I realize, this is the inevitable truth–

The transient existence of mankind,

and sure my days were dropping down.

But then should I mourn, should I weep over this ship of life

that is sure to sink one day?

No, I am the sailor, I should stay strong.

There is time neither to dwell in the fading past,

nor to let unease grow over the impending future.

Just like the sand in shades of amber, moving between the past and future

I've got a journey right at the moment and no one can grab me off my present.

This voyage, I've got to make it worthwhile, savour it with a tint of uniqueness.

Fix my sails through the raging storms and rise up cutting the guardian knot.

The hourglass stood on the table top, steady and stable as it has for ages.

The sand grains sparkled in hazel tan as the sunlight speared through the weathered glass.

How are Bed Looks

by Priya Kulkarni

The bed is sprawled with,

Her tresses all across me,

Her legs tucked under mine,

Closely cuddled in my arms.

Her safest place of all,

Her warm skin against mine,

Her fragrance mixed with mine,

The way our bed holds us

As, if it know

That She is a world,

Of my only own.

Cry

by Kunika Rawlani

I cry,

To let my feelings dry.

I cry even on a little reason,

Because they mean a ton.

Not all those who cry are girls,

We forget; man too have emotions.

Crying is actually good for health,

A human can cry; even though he had accumulated wealth.

For me, crying means to let out,

So from next time cry without a doubt.

Snowfall

by Ethan Chinnery

Snowfalls gently outside our little cabin in the woods,

The air was still as if time had frozen in the harsh winter,

Leaving only us snuggled together.

Bed haired and bundled with a blanket,

Cinnamon and nutmeg wafting from our Christmas hot chocolate.

Your soft content smile, sending butterflies through me,

Like the autumn we first met.

Every day I fall,

Like snow,

Like those autumn leaves,

Forever for you.

Muliebrity

by Laiba Sohail

Her eyes are sharp but not arrogant,

Her stance is strong but not hard,

Her smile is calculated but not one of distaste.

She's beautiful but not a show-off,

Her hands are soft but not too soft to carry the load.

She's a woman who's firm inside out,

Not known for her charms; but for the wit,

A survival of the fittest.

Conceit

by Laiba Sohail

Hail the work of the craftsman,

Praise his skills all through the town

In a loud pleased voice,

So that, every towns man shall know his name,

But don't let it reach the doors of the said artisans,

For I fear if he hears his name being chanted

Knows of the plaudit.

His work might contaminate,

His hands might hesitate,

Making another masterpiece.

I Wish to Create a Monster

by Christian Scully

I wish to create a monster

So void of self

That emptiness fills it.

That silence, screams in its wake

I wish to create a monster,

That causes stillness to shudder,

That causes deafness to wince at its roar

That knows no limit.

That is endless.

That enslaves, enraptures, and envelopes everything

And I will name it love.

Fallen

by Deeksha Raina

Once upon a time,

a seed was planted,

with utmost care and tenderness.

Gradually as the bud bloomed,

the floral was stroked lightly,

love transpired in the water droplets.

Until,

This particular branch,

was twisted towards the end,

trying to pave a different path,

only to be held back,

by the roots of it's trunk.

There ensued a struggle,

However rough the branch,

the flower was weaving its own story,

Alas!

It's petals now entangled,

in the obligation of their love,

It's dreams were swallowed,

by the moulding of those fingers,

It's spirit engulfed,

in the softness of those palms.

The flower suffocated,

in the air that was set,

It couldn't live,

with the stigma that it now carried,

It drooped down,

as its stalk stood broken from within.

The flower had fallen,

It's happiness now scattered,

in the ashes so formed.

You Can Be You

by Prakriti Batra

You're alive

For what you behold inside.

A drug, that you're holding onto.

Something that you're feeding on

Nothing you can't do,

Nothing you can't give up on.

Feeling what you want to

Being what you are

Pretending is the new normal

Start being informal

For whatever you have

Will help you build more

Thoughts create emotions,

Mistakes create experiences.

Procrastinating won't help

Push yourself for more.

Feel it now

Tomorrow isn't for sure.

What's outside? The pandemic.

Inside? The thoughts.

It's all a blessing, you'll only know when it's the last

Like the wind touches the ocean

Your mind touches your soul.

Graveyard to Heaven

by Ruchika Sharma

Quilted and dead down upon grey,

Gazing sapphire-blue day,

Nugatory roots of dry petal,

Universe is a painting of William Havel,

Counting breath with cold zephyr,

Wow! What an amusing weather!

Ashes and gloom around,

Glee to fill the wound,

Days to months to year,

Smile broadens from cheek to ear,

One day, to touch the sky,

Only hope in her eye.

Oh Almighty! What a miracle!

Saplings are growing without an obstacle,

Oh Tulip! So bright to glow,

A beautiful Aurora Borealis show,

Purple, Red, White, Pink,

Showering Love, Royalty, Happiness's ink,

She's at zenith of Seven to Eleven,

Burgeon From Graveyard to Heaven.

The Marital Love

by Deeksha Raina

I was only nineteen,

He dressed me in jade green,

Had I been able to foresee,

I wouldn't have agreed to be his queen.

We got married in the town hall,

He treated me like a doll,

He was there at my beck and call,

First few months were like waltz in a ball,

His love was a fireball.

I wonder why it changed then,

I wonder when we became estranged,

How suddenly I was visited by different men,

All, who had a vested interest,

I wonder when I had become so insignificant,

How my happiness was now indifferent.

Days are cold and nights always warm,

My body is now a money plant,

I am left blindfold and my voice is choked,

Their lust is many a times uncontrolled,

Once I cried and received a black eye,

Since then, I bid my dreams goodbye.

He says people will believe his lies,

Society will say I am his legally wedded wife,

You'll say husband is always right,

Won't You.

Don't you say this to countless women,

Who are suffering at the hands of ruthless men?

Is Someone There?

by Madhurya Kommuri

My hands sweat,

My heart aches,

My body it shakes.

But is someone there?

Who even care?

Sometimes my eyes rain,

Succumbing to this pain.

To the demons in my mind I'm chained.

But is someone there?

Who even care?

I pull myself near,

Trembling with fear.

My silent cries which no body hear.

But is someone there

Who even care?

What about the times when it's,

Not my eyes but my heart that bleeds,

Into depths of trauma it leads,

And I'm left quite indeed.

But is someone there?

Who even care?

My room doors I close,

Laying numb on the floor,

Crying more and more.

But is someone there?

Who even care?

This agony it kills,

I gulp many pills,

Oh, God! Like hell, it feels.

But is someone there?

Who even care?

There are wounds so deep,

Which I myself am afraid to peep,

And this to myself I keep.

But is someone there?

Who even care?

On papers, walls I scrabble,

Wanting myself to strangle,

With pain, I struggle,

Life or death – what to choose,

Fed up and my control I lose.

But is someone there?

Who even care?

My strength as a prey to the sorrow it bends,

To kill myself my heart tends.

Only if there's someone to befriend,

whose ears they could lend,

My wounds would definitely mend.

But is someone there?

Who even care?

Is someone there?

Who really care?

Someone when I dial,

To stay a little while,

Walk the extra mile,

To bring back my smile?

Oh wait... let me ask

Can you be that someone..?

Your smile can make someone's day brighter,

The time you spend can make their heart lighter.

Love, care, kindness– they have a great power,

Never underestimate,

Trust me you can change lives forever.

So why not...

Let's shout out

Hey beautiful soul,

I know in your heart there is a hole.

But let's not make it a big deal,

I promise to help you heal.

It's not a big matter,

Things will eventually get better.

Forget your fears,

I'll be there to wipe your tears.

It's alright,

Don't give in to your plight,

You can defeat the devils in your fight,

Because you, my dear

Are a warrior with might!

And some day to the world proudly,

You'd say "I am victorious" loudly !

Faith in Ownself

by Vaishnavi Singh

A globe full of consolidation,

My dear! WAIT, PAUSE and THINK.....

You are nonpareil in any situation.

Other Mortals are better,

But in their interests...

You are the one who has courage,

Courage to amour your own self,

And let their evil intent go vague......

Standstill, and be obdurate,

They will decimate.....

But you will not stop and wait,

Intent is high let these fellow respite your moral....

Oh dear! Love your ardour,

And let them dismal,

Time is there stay strong,

And never let your vehemence,

Be your halt.....

Be Like Water

by Sehaf Haq

My mother once told me,

A girl must be like water,

adjust and fit in everywhere she goes.

I said,

Yes I will be like water,

drown those who disturb my tide,

give life to those who tread gently.

My mother once told me,

A girl must be like water,

adjust and fit in with any man she marries.

I said,

Yes I will be like water,

slip away from between his fingers every time he tries to control me,

overflow from his house every time he tells me to stay indoors.

My mother once told me,

A girl must be like water,

adjust and adapt to every situation she's put in.

I said,

Yes I will be like water,

but I would not water a dead garden,

nor would I water a weedy garden.

Always and Forever

by Pranshi Singal

Your love hurts

your love consumes

please find me a way

to let you go

because every path I take

leads me to you

each day, each hour, each minute

I just can't keep my heart shut

please find me a way

to put those feelings away

please don't turn your back

your love is all I lack

please find me a way

to stop thinking of you

because every dream I have

is all about you

but just remember this thing

this love is more than just a fling

that feeling of your love

I just can't kill

but it seems like

I've come to a conclusion

I love you,

always have, will till eternity.

Duality of Virtue

by Rashi Aggarwal

Proud over his fictitious virtue,

To what extent is this mind-set true

Convincing himself to society's anatomy

It's nothing but a mere dichotomy

Between the morals and soul

Fighting to get the idea as a whole

Perception is taken to be misleading

Quieting the greatest minds by pleading

"right to the expression" they say

Opinion should be taken righteous

Believing in the superiority of their virtue

Then why iniquity flows in you

Virtue is nothing but

A farrago of mysticism and dualism

Where the mind works as a prism

Moralities refracted as paradoxes.

The Unknown Path

by Deeksha Raina

Have you been to that part of the town?

Where needs have known to be long aroused,

The lane which is usually frowned upon,

And her muffled screams are drowned by dawn...

Have you gone during the bright lit night?

When men find delight and women are a sight,

The rooms are nothing but airtight,

It's famously known for its red lights!

Her life is void of all the colours

Red and Black is all that matters,

Those pouncing on the outside have bloodshot eyes,

What's left in the inside is dark and blind.

Homecoming

by C.L. Williams

The maker called, he's ready for me to come home,

I just wanted you, you'll never be alone.

I have much to tell you, I'm not guaranteed tomorrow,

The maker has called, my time here is now borrowed.

One thing I must tell you, always believe

I know it will be difficult since I'm about to leave.

But you have to be strong, at least for the others

For the family, even your sisters and brothers.

If I only have time to say one thing, I know it would be,

No matter what, I don't want you to cry for me.

I know you'll want to since my time here is through,

You'll understand better when the maker is ready for you.

So I say this, do not cry because my time here is done,

Because my life isn't over, it's only just begun.

I

by Deeksha Raina

"*You are strong enough, you're the one who is tough!*"

Oh, I am sorry to rebuff you,

Maybe, just maybe, I can easily bluff!

I seek appreciation, I harbour secret temptations,

I look all decked up, but inside I am wrecked up,

I am not perfect, I have got that checked up!

My thirst is your nod of approval,

All I want is your applaud,

Isn't my existence flawed?

I know you will never admire,

I know my hopes will backfire,

Yet, I am here, playing with fire!

No, dear, I am not strong.

You've got me all wrong,

Because I don't really belong,

Not for long; long past the furlong.

I Can't Explain

by Joe King

I can't explain my brain today,

There's too much pain, it's safe to say.

It's too insane to fade away,

I can't sustain that brain today.

I can't explain this pain today,

That mental strain, it came to stay.

Like crack cocaine which raids my brain,

I can't sustain that pain again.

I can't explain the rain today,

It chose my brain, then rained away.

And once it came, it came to stay,

I can't sustain that rain today.

If, I explained my brain today,

And all the pain that came my way.

Would you not stay to save my day?

But run away to save your fate,

If you asked me, I'd always stay.

The Hollow Millennials

by Laiba Sohail

Disoriented minds,

Scratched faces,

Incomplete smiles,

Shallow eyes,

Empty words...

That's all I see,

That's the only picture my eyes are able to form,

That's the only picture my heart is able to see,

Of the people around me.

Ubiquity

by John McCafferty

Be who you see further in time,

Search along the beaten path.

Higher self in mind,

Opportunities arise,

Recurring dreams and themes,

of stepping stones with deeper tones.

Echoes passed from distant lives,

Duality is a cyclical sign,

When life seems finite.

The Truth of this World

by Sehaf Haq

As the clouds stop crying, and the skies stop glooming,

when the soil is fragranced, and the flowers start blooming,

a spectrum of colours creeps into the sky's pallor,

and of orange you comment, 'But that's not a real colour!'

You tell me, 'It's only but a mix of yellow and red.'

'But that's how everyone in this world is,' I said.

We never call upon anyone by what they are like,

we always call upon them by what they look like.

A person of colour is beneath your white skin,

and if they're black, then their only place is the bin.

A person who shows skin is not worthy of respect,

yet a person who covers is a suspicious subject.

If a man is wrong, even then he's never wrong,

and if a woman is wrong, then she's always wrong.

Such is the truth of this world we live in,

we judge not by what is, we judge by what has been.

Memory Card

by Manaswi Patil

My beloved memory card,

Words of gratitude with regards,

For saving the moments of my life,

All those sweet and strive.

The flashback prevails,

Remembers me my childhood plays.

The stories so lame,

Fitted in a frame.

Pictures of school days,

The thoughts that render me awake.

Those beautiful moments cherished,

Saved as memories today.

It is simply,

A closet of evocation.

Able to rewind,

Pause and play my emotions.

A tiny chip hoarding,

A chock-full of warmth,

With hugs twirled and twisted.

This little chip in my head,

Keeps me alive when I'm dead.

Women

by Madhurya Kommuri

Yes, I wear a gown!

But when you put me down,

Don't expect me to stay calm.

I'll fight,

With all my might,

For it is my right!

With my courage,

I'll show you that the image in your head,

About me (women) is just a mirage.

I'll no more cry,

Till the tears dry.

You'll see my rage,

Breaking the cage.

I'll no longer play according to your dice,

Spreading my wings, you'll see me rise.

Wearing my womanhood as a crown,

I'll never frown!

Yes, I bleed,

And that is my power indeed!

Yes, I wear a gown,

And nobody can put me down!

How Great

by Jagruthi Kommuri

How great is the creation,

That it reminds us the supremacy of the Creator;

How blessed are humans to feel something and be able to explain the emotion,

That it helps us realize we are nothing but a handy work of the Creator;

How the world works, this does not end in an explanation,

But it surely makes us discern the presence of the Creator;

Who are we to feel significant and live this generation?

Nothing but to praise how magnificent is the glory of the Creator.

The Devil

by Deeksha Raina

Eyes open, wake up and smile.

Sleep plays hide and seek,

Reality is clouding my eyes,

Dreams drowning in the depths of darkness.

Turning and tossing inevitably,

My screams are chained into rosy sheets.

Cold passes over on the hottest nights,

Bearing its weight, heaviness seeps into my soul,

Until I face the beast in the eye.

A double-edged sword, the demon leaves me shocked,

As Harvey Dent comes into focus, I search frantically for my Batman.

Right side painted in burn, mocking yet tempting me

wrong, oops left side plays it safe, begging me to join in.

This is no more the bogeyman,

As the clock hands tick at six,

It's the devil incarnate, his laughter echoing through my veins.

Pleading, crying out in anguish

His silence in deafening, engulfing my wails,

Slowly, I give in, into the abyss of the devil,

The devil called Life.

Eyes open, wake up and smile.

The Woman

by Deeksha Raina

I see her,

a woman, naked

her eyes staring deep

into the white washed roof.

Her palms bared over her torso,

bony shoulders stroke the ground beneath,

and a smile, slow and almost dispassionate

fleetingly comes and goes.

Lain and open, her scars are

displayed across herself,

for you to judge or pity,

oh! Only if she could care any less.

I see her,

a woman, dangerous

as she has risen

from the flames of truth,

her own truth

broken free,

from the chains of society

and I smile,

as the queen conquers all.

Wilde Girl

by Ethan Chinnery

Fairy Floss Hair,

Words just as sweet,

You make me want to come up for air,

Not drown in these seas,

Future bright as bright can be,

Hidden behind eyes of storm summer breeze,

For one day I shall meet her,

By the flowers and the sea,

Where the brightest star she shall be,

Alas, I stand alone by the sea.

Draped in melancholy,

for those with eyes to see.

Oh! Wilde Girl, Why have you forsaken me?

Perhaps one day we can stand together by the flowers and the sea.

How I dream for her be the brightest star she can be.

The Boy that the Robin Killed

by Manoj Vaz

The boy crouched behind the oak tree,

His catapult ready to stone.

Taking baby steps from child to man,

He was ready to break free.

The robin had seen the boy at play,

Often in the woods before.

Had no fear of coming in his way,

And found no reason to soar.

The robin fluffed himself against the cold,

And sang like he usually sang.

The boy, a hunter now, brave and bold,

Drew back the bands, took aim and twang!

The stone sped and did not err,

Accurate, hard and strong,

It crashed through the feathers,

And broke the robin's song.

The boy, a killer now, flung the weapon,

Forgetting right from wrong,

With misplaced joy all along,

Saw red feathers scatter there upon.

Broken, battered, the robin lying dead,

The boy picked up the shattered bird.

Emotions surging through him wouldn't rest,

He smoothened the robin's chest.

Suddenly, a new sound now,

Cut into the boy's despair.

For in the branches of a lower bough,

A nest of tiny robins crying there.

And through the years that lay ahead,

It remained alive in times of grief and joy,

The story of the robin, dead,

A crime that killed a young boy.

It's Just You, Me and Our Hug

by Keshav Dev Tiwari

When I feel like crying,

I seek your arms,

your love comes to me,

and make me warm.

When I miss you

the most,

perhaps you became

my problem's host.

I don't know

what makes it

so special,

but every time,

I see you,

I feel like,

My true love

Proposal.

It never came to

say Goodbye,

your vibes, oh! Yes,

I'm taking of your eyes.

You are my,

the most

beautiful dream

I promise,

You'll always be

been my only queen.

When it comes

for my life bugs,

I always wish for you

and there,

it's just you, me

and our hug....

Fly Like an Eagle

by Joe King

I know that insults can be cruel,

But don't except them big or small.

Just treat them like a ping-pong ball,

That's bouncing off a strong brick wall.

You are that wall that guards your soul,

It's filled with love that makes you whole.

It guards from hate, as love's your goal,

That's who you are, that's how you roll.

If you encounter someone's hate,

Just block them out, don't take the bait.

Don't even try to set them straight,

Just say "Goodbye", then you'll do great.

Immerse yourself with loving people,

who cheer you up, and treat you equal.

Don't follow those who delve in evil,

You're not a sheep like all those sheeple.

It's Not About

by Joe King

It's not about the clothes you wear,

Or even how you style your hair,

The reason girl that you are rare,

is down to how much love you share,

It's not about the way you look,

Or just how badly you can't cook,

We'd learn together through a book,

No matter how much time it took.

It's not about your lack of glory,

Or if your past is grim and gory,

I'm just glad that you adore me,

So tell me girl your every story,

But only tell me if you're sure,

I don't mind if you're insecure,

It's not like I am keeping score,

It's just I'd like to know you more,

The way I feel for you is pure.

Kundalini

by John McCafferty

Om,

Clear the mind

with forms of breath control,

Vibrations emanate,

Serpent flows in swirls,

It curls around the center line,

Seven points along the spine,

From base to crown,

Varied hues are queued,

Where energy is key,

Use the force,

to elevate your qi.

Need of Life

by Priya Kulkarni

A little peace, a little spice,

A little sweet, a little sour,

A little wet, a little dry,

We belong to us, we forget this first,

Giving everything to others, makes no sense henceforth

Live a little, love a little,

The one who was your downfall, can never bring you your best.

Don't leave, just leave the past,

Walk in the present, looking at the end is the bright future.

In this War, Without You

by Snehal Agarwal

Every morning without you makes me weak,
And every night it gets harder to sleep,

The scorching heat reminds me of your cool eyes,
And the lonely afternoons, of the painful goodbyes,

I imagine you caressing my hair,
Shooing away my nightmares,

In this war against humanity,
We maintain distance to preserve our sanity,

Oh how much I want to be with you,
To love you, without caring about the invisible enemy.

Thank you for reading Midnight Writers!
We hope that you have enjoyed these beautiful poems written by
such talented authors.

The few next pages are a creative space for you where you will find some interesting activities. Once you have completed them, you can click a picture of your creative space and share it on social media with the hashtag #midnightwriters. Don't forget to tag Inkfeathers Publishing in your posts. We'd love to hear from you!

***Which poem did you like best from this book? What feelings
did that poem evoke for you ?***

Scribble any random quote, poem or a micro-tale.

Draw some random doodles or shapes to describe how you feel at this moment!

ABOUT THE AUTHORS

Rashi Agarwal

Rashi Agarwal is an International business graduate from New Delhi. Her passion for art and culture got her interested in reading classics and contemporary fiction, study art and classical dance. She fulfils herself through writing and working for animal welfare.

Sushma Chaudhary

Sushma Chaudhary, a girl who got the eyes of innocence, the face of an angel, a personality of a dreamer and a smile that hides more mysteries than one can ever imagine. She has been an educator for five years. She loves to get lost in the world of imagination just by reading novels. She finds her second home in the books. Writing makes her feel comfortable and unburdens her mind. Her writing can be found on Instagram at @its_me0602. She is writing her own story and hopefully will release her book soon.

Anushka Shah

Anushka Shah is a Chartered Accountant by profession and a Deloitte Consultant. Writing is her way of expressing herself. She started writing at a young age and has been an avid reader as well. She mostly writes for herself but has recently expanded her horizons towards the people, to spread a solid message through her words.

Arshveen Behr

Arshveen Behr is a 17-year-old ambivert. Writing has been her passion since the time she knew that she could confide in words and they'll never break her trust. Books were her hideout and she is totally a couch potato. A quote that keeps her going is 'If you're going through hell, keep going. Why would you stop in hell?' And that's that. You can find her on Instagram at @kaurwrites_

Manoj Vaz

Manoj is an advertising copywriter with 3 decades of experience handling over 50 blue-chip clients. He has published three books; Tinsel - a hard look at Mumbai's Show Biz, The Kidnapping, and the Meth Mystery - both part of the Magic Chest Series for teenagers.

Tanvi Kulkarni

Writing is not just a passion but a modicum of bringing change in our world. Tanvi Kulkarni, writes out her heart and the earnest feelings in it honestly. She believes that no topic is too risky, too cliché, too deep or too light to write about. That being said, one of the reasons of writing for her is feeling the rush of ink and scratch of the pencil on the paper. Even her fellow readers know about the enamouring smell and feel of paper. Reading a lot of classical literature, wonderful world of fantasy, facts that bring to light the state of our world made her involuntarily start to write. Hoping to entice you with her strongly felt and lovingly worded creations for a long time.

Priya Kulkarni

Priya Kulkarni is an IT professional working with an MNC. Her passions include writing poetry, painting and singing. She is also an excellent baker. Her poetry touches hearts with a delicate and subtle sense of feelings. She creates magic with words and her art work. She invokes beautiful feelings within, whispering poems about life, love and human relationships. She also touches horror. Her #HeShe stories are quite popular and are wonderful to read.

Her expertise with art is both acrylic and watercolours paintings. Her art can be found on her Instagram profile @uncanny_piscean. Her wide range of poems are published on her Instagram at @chitchat.collectibles. Her short stories can be found on her website at www.prettypiscean.com.

Sehaf Haq

Sehaf Haq is a 23-year-old, 5th year medical student from Jeddah, Saudi Arabia. While her ambition is to be a successful doctor, her passion is to be a bestselling author. She began writing poetry five years ago, when her mind

became too small to hold her volatile thoughts. She is an ardent Harry Potter fan and absolutely adores kittens.

Jagruthi Kommuri

K. Jagruthi is an E-commerce graduate, and a writer by chance who loves to write to ignite a little hope and faith in the reader. She's a simple girl who finds solace in words and writes to spread love & positivity to the world. She believes kindness goes a long way when communicated through heart.

Saniya Rumazia

In a world of dark wisdom and romance, she usually like to contribute her thoughts through the web of poetry, which makes perfect sense. Legend says that she checks Calvin and Hobbes comic strips to decode the deeper mysteries of life. Saniya Rumazia is an impulsive student who has a thing for good ol' fashioned letters and pressed flowers.

Padmini Peteri

Padmini Peteri has a Post Graduate in literature from Osmania University and PG Diploma in ELT from EFL University. She has a passion for reading and writing. She writes short stories and poetry in both English and Hindi. Her writings find wings in her Instagram handle minithoughts_pp. To her writing is healing. She believes in smiling and spreading happiness as it makes the world a better place to live in.

Madhurya Kommuri

Madhurya Kommuri is an aspiring psychologist by profession and a poet by passion. A perfect imperfection, a beautiful mess; is what defines her the best. Bringing out the stories people bury inside with patience and comforting with soothing poetry is her way of bringing peace to minds and making world a better place to live.

Joe King

Joe King is from Bournemouth which is on the south coast of England. Writing for him is a therapy and a way of expression. It helps him to express his truest deepest emotions and anxiety as well. He loves to write to inspire others with rhyming poetry that

flows. If he can brighten up one person's day or inspire them in some sort of way with his words then that is enough for him and will give him great satisfaction. Life is a journey and we all have a story to tell and poetry is a huge part of his journey. He feels so blessed to have such a gift that he can share with readers and he is even more blessed to have the most amazing family anyone could ever wish for.

Prakriti Batra

Prakriti Batra is a working individual and likes to observe things in a broader perspective. Apart from work, she likes singing and writing poems. She has always been encouraged and appreciated for her way of writing. We all know what we are good at, because it comes from within the heart.

Mrinalini Singh

Mrinalini Singh is currently pursuing Masters in Sports Management and plays football. Writing has always been a secret passion she barely spoke to anyone about until now. Her writings are inspired from her day to day life.

Shrishail Bhurke

Shrishail Bhurke is a song writer, student and a writer from Karnataka. He usually likes to write about silent and blind love stories. He believes that poems speak about the charm, grief and all those hidden emotions behind our lids.

The real beauty lies in those eyes, what they seek is just a mystery and majesty to explore. Though you hide many things but, your eyes reveal them all.

Keshav Dev Tiwari

Keshav Dev Tiwari is a writer by heart and an extrovert as a person. Most of the people who have some special quality or special talent in them use it for their own good. But he wanted to use his words for others, he wanted to write what others feel and can relate to.

Pranshi Singal

Pranshi Singal, a teenager who started writing as a hobby, lives in New Delhi, India. She loves reading, listening to music, and traveling. She is an aspiring writer who believes in a world full of wonder, magic, and love.

Laiba Sohail

Laiba Sohail is an insightful writer. Her writings are based on instinctive abilities in understanding human emotions and behaviours. Being only 17 years of age and a second-year student, she surprises the readers with her expression on a variety of experiences. Study of Psychology as a subject, fondness for literature, quest for history and observation of politics makes her a dynamic writer. She has always been passionate for creative arts in her school and college, an ardent reader and a confident speaker. Her maiden book of poetry is in the process of publication.

John McCafferty

John McCafferty, C5/6 Tetraplegic wheelchair user from a spinal cord injury in 2003. He completed his B.A. (Hons) and M.A. in Photography at Middlesex University 2007-11. At present he is the CEO of an accessible arts charity www.communityfocus.co.uk He started writing poetry in January 2020 as a form of reflection on day to day observations. Loosely using writing as a tool has opened different parts of his brain to communicate and been beneficial in approaching some of life's hurdles as opportunities instead.

Utkarsh Pandey

Utkarsh Pandey is a full-time investment Banker based out of Pune, India. He likes singing and song writing. He realised his inclination towards writing in the year 2018 and started writing often with the passing time. He started off with simple  motivational sentences and later it blossomed into writing poems and short stories.

Deeksha Raina

 An avid reader, a passionate artist and a writer in the making, her first stint with her pen started at the age of 15 and ever since, there has been no looking back. Reading started off as just a hobby, but over the years, it made her realise that writing was her real passion and that's what eventually fuelled her dream of becoming an author. After publishing her first novel titled- 'It Was Love', she is now venturing deeper into penning

down her thoughts, ranging from poetry to free verses, both in English and Hindi languages.

Purva Mestry Ingale

Purva Mestry Ingale is a French teacher by profession but also an avid reader, a movie buff, a lover of nature and an imaginator. She has always been passionate towards writing and started writing at the age of 12. It started with poems and slowly she moved on to write stories and essays too. She has been publishing on her blog (www.talltales1.wordpress.com) on and off since the past eight years now. Her blog was featured on Baggout as one of the top 15 creative writing blogs in India. She has also been awarded as Literary Colonel on storymirror.com.

Recently, she has started a dedicated Instagram account for her writing @tallertales1. She tries to portray a deeper perspective into everyday things and aims at creating a change through it. A believer in spreading positivity, she wants to use her writing to do so.

Ethan Chinnery

Ethan Chinnery is a 23-year-old man who lives in rural Australia and spends a lot of time hanging out with his pet rabbits: Buttons and Pumpernickel. He has been into poetry for about four years now and it started out mainly while he was just playing with  words. He aims to write short stories and maybe novels at some point in life.

Kristina Kerber

 Artemis, also named as Krissi offline, which sounds considerably less mysterious and substantially more practical. Poetry has accompanied her for many years now – which makes her sound a lot older than 20 years. She has discovered that writing stories is her own way of exploring her innermost feelings as well as the world around her.

For her, writing has always felt as if words and images were simply invading her mind and pouring out of her fingertips onto the paper which usually translates to fanatical typing on the mobile. If you enjoy her work and are interested in catching a glimpse of her mind, she welcomes you to visit her Instagram page- @alliterative_artemis

Vaishnavi Singh

Vaishnavi Singh is a Law student. She loves the legal field as there are so many things related to one's daily life, society and you tranquil many new things here every day. She believes that one should live life "to express and not to impress" and this is what makes her write. She writes what she feels. For her, letters are the best gift to express emotions and feelings. She is an extrovert and loves to explore life. She firmly believes that life is not a competitive platform rather it's a beautiful thing to live and feel.

Kunika Rawlani

Kunika Rawlani originally resides in Ulhasnagar, Maharashtra. Currently, she is pursuing her CA. Writing is a dearest friend of her which she got to realise one and a half years ago. She never gets tired of writing, thinking and sleeping.

Nandana Nataraj

Nandana Nataraj is an IT professional who finds her latibule in words. She loves to retreat to the cocoon of her thoughts and string them to verses and poetry. She started her journey by scribbling tiny poems in her little diary which she used

to then carry as a treasure box and loved reading it to others. She loves to jot down things that touch her soul as little as they can be, her feelings, epiphanies and perspectives. She firmly believes in the art of tingeing souls with a splash of ink and spreading hues of positivity and inspiration through her works.

Christian Scully

Christian Scully is based in Brixham Devon UK. Writer, poet and a musician he is inspired by the people of his daily commutes to and from work, as well as the general chaos of modern life. He hopes to complete his first collection ‘Commuter Musing’ by the end of 2020.

Ruchika Sharma

Ruchika Sharma is an aspiring science student and perpetual lover of exploring history. She is from "City of Temples", Jammu. She takes up writing as a creative journey of self-discovery. She loves to express through a pen despite being an introvert most often. She loves to travel, explore historical places and she is a great admirer of nature and pet lover too. Love, Nature, Societal norms, Feminism and Patriotism are the essence of her poetries. She is a co-author of various anthologies. She wants to bring a wave of change in the minds of youth "By Her Pen".

Alexandra Michelle

To Alexandra Michelle, expressing herself through creation brings her so much peace and solace. She is a curious person and all art forms impact her deeply. Her poetry comes straight from her heart; so, it is raw, authentic, and true to her experiences in life. She has created her own Instagram page with the intention of healing through a healthy outlet. She hopes to bring comfort to others as she has received from the wonderful poetry community.

C.L. Williams

C.L. Williams is an International Bestselling Author living in Central Virginia. He's written eight poetry books, five novellas, one novel, and is a contributor to a multitude of anthologies. His previous poetry book The Paradox Complex features the poem "Sad Crying Clown" that was turned into a short film by Matthew Mark Hunter of MMH Productions and is available to watch on the MMH Productions' YouTube channel. He is currently releasing a series of novelettes under the banner Chaos Fusion. C.L. Williams is currently working on his newest poetry book OMNI- and Bed Bugs, a supplement book to the MMH productions film of the same name.

Fiza Meghrajiya

Fiza Meghrajiya considers writing as her passion which keeps her mind and heart happy. She is going to become an engineer soon. She loves to motivate people and likes to take inspiration from every little thing that surrounds her. You may also find her on Instagram @wordsofshygirl_

Manaswi Patil

Manaswi Patil is a student from Karnataka, India. She writes poems, quotes and shayaris as she loves picturing her emotions in front of the readers. The chock-full of memories prevailing into her mind made her write this poem. The poem Memory Card is such a tiny thing hoarding all her treasures, sweetest moments, heartfelt memories and all the warmth and love.

Snehal Agarwal

Snehal Agarwal is a 21-year-old Chartered Accountant from Mumbai. She is talkative, a sitcom fanatic and secretly a nerd. Writing allowed her to express her emotions on the topics she feels strongly about and has always given her a sense of power to bring a change in the society. She has been writing since a long time now but it's only recently that she decided to share it with the world.

Dr. Apteena Johnson Kakkadu

Dr. Apteena Johnson Kakkadu is a dentist and a writer. Her debut book was LORD OF THE WORDS vol-1. She originally belongs to Kerala, India.

OUR STORY

We're all on a Journey, and our "Writers" have made it Beautiful.

A dreamcatcher is an object made with feathers and strings, essentially used as lucky charms in many parts of the world. The same way, Inkfeathers brings together writers, editors, and artists together to form a dreamcatcher that works in favour for the young writers and readers and if you're positive about it, it may bring you luck as well.

We at Inkfeathers are connected to thousands of writers globally, who believe in the magic of telling stories. This stream of connectivity with the writers, the fact that everyone has a unique detail or edge to their story makes Inkfeathers proud to partner with these young literary as well as collaborative minds.

Back in 2013, our founders came together to form an offline group for their love of literature, and this formed collaborative energy with many young literature-wounded minds which eventually led these offline meetings to stand-ups, storytelling events, poetry slams, meet-ups to share experiences and many others. In 2016, Inkfeathers finally launched as the brand project under one Private Limited Company. This expanded opportunity gave a number of possibilities and a new way to expand our support for writers.

This dream of wanting to bring together writers as well as readers has come true beyond measure as writers connect to us from countries like United States, United Kingdom, Canada each day to bring their stories to life.

As of this year, we are extremely delighted to provide you our website (www.inkfeathers.com) where all your queries can be resolved about our self-publishing process and latest anthologies. You can get hold of the latest updates on anthologies, events, offers, new book releases and so much more here. You can go ahead and order a book from our bookstore to get a taste of our mindful curation of stories and poems.

Inkfeathers Publishing family encourages you to really put your feelings out there in words for the world to see, in order to have a common ground to grow mutually. We are a creative platform for all those seeking literary help in terms of having their words published.

Believe us, publishing a book is not easy, but we come to a writer's rescue at each phase of having their book in print in terms of Editing, Designing, Branding, Marketing and all the other work that goes behind until you have a printed copy in your hands for Distribution. Together, it couldn't have been any easier. We will be there for you, to help you turn your manuscript into a freshly bound book that sells off the glass bookshelves.

With Love,
Inkfeathers Publishing

OTHER PUBLISHED BOOKS

Hope And Beyond- A Journey Through Mental Health

This book brings some stories of warriors; some real, some fictional who fought an unseen battle, not with a living monster but with something more powerful, our own mind and body. The world is closing and what is most important is to open up to yourself and to have faith in the warm hugs you receive on your way. This book wants to test that power of sharing and test the strength in the stories of acknowledging the heavy and hazy days. Testing our or our dear one's emotional health and we want to embrace and hear the journeys, long or short, it doesn't matter until you have not given up.

**Scan the QR Code
To order your copy.**

Little Occult Affairs- Untold Mysteries Unfold

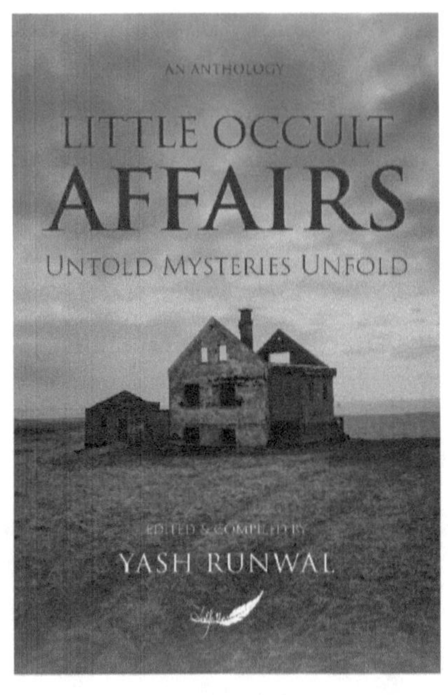

Taking you on some unplanned, mystical journeys into this realm of 23 beautifully mysterious minds. This anthology has everything it takes to keep you flipping through pages trying to envisage each writer's mind and experience life, death, secrets, darkness and so much more as you dive deep in it, making you feel like you live the story itself. The assortment and diversity of the co-authors assure of taking you to the edge of your senses while experiencing each story. With each page, Untold Mysteries Unfold.

**Scan the QR Code
To order your copy.**

INKFEATHERS PUBLISHING

India's Most Author Friendly Publishing House

Stay updated about latest anthologies, events, exclusive offers, contests, product giveaways and other things that we do to support authors.

 Inkfeathers Publishing

 @InkfeathersPublishing

 @_Inkfeathers

 @Inkfeathers

 Inkfeathers.com

We'd love to connect with you!

9 788819 461996 3